ANIMAL DIARIES

Lion

STEVE PARKER

QEB

Copyright © QEB Publishing 2014

First published in the United States in 2014 by
QEB Publishing, Inc.
3 Wrigley, Suite A
Irvine, CA 92618
www.qed-publishing.co.uk

A CIP record for this book is available from the Library of Congress.

ISBN 978 1 60992 615 1

Project Editor Carey Scott
Illustrator Peter David Scott/The Art Agency
Designer Dave Ball
QED Project Editor Tasha Percy
Managing Editor Victoria Garrard
Design Manager Anna Lubecka

Printed and bound in China

Photo Credits
Corbis Fotofeeling/Westend61 p23; **Nature plc** Ole Jorgen Liodden p22;
Shutterstock Andreas Doppelmayr p11, Eric Isselee p18, John Michael
Evan Potter p29, Pal2iyawit p15; Gordan, David M. Scrader, Luminis,
Oleg Golovnev, Ana de Sousa, Valentin Agapov, Dementeva, Petr Jilek
all background images

Contents

My tongue almost reaches my mane!

My Pride

It's another mega-hot day on the East African savanna. Most grown-ups in My Pride are resting or asleep. We all laze around here until dusk. Then, when it's cooler, the Moms get ready for the Hunt.

Lion (male)

Group Mammals—carnivores

Adult length 10 feet including tail

Weight 485 pounds

Habitat Grassland, bush, open woodland

Food Wildebeest, zebra, buffalo, small gazelle, eland (antelope), and warthog

Features Large hairy mane around neck and shoulders, long sharp teeth, dark tail-tuft, loud roar

Other Dad is second in command.

Big Sis dozing.

I'm cuddling up with My Mom.

The cubs want to play, but it's just too tiring in this heat. Anyway, I'm getting too big to mess around with those babies. Today is my second birthday. I'm growing up fast!

4

My labels show who's who in My Pride. We're like one big happy family. Not like last year when New Dad came and chased away Old Dad, took charge, and killed the two smallest cubs! More on that later . . .

More on that later . . .

LION HUNGER LEVEL

STARVING
Severe risk of lion attack

VERY HUNGRY
High risk of lion attack

HUNGRY
General risk of lion attack

FULL
Low risk of lion attack

This chart shows how much of a threat My Pride is, based on how hungry we are.

New Dad is big and fierce. He's the boss!

Second Mom is My Mom's younger sister.

Young Cousin wants to play.

5

Savanna Friends

When I was little, I stayed by My Mom's side. Now that I'm bigger, I can explore on my own. Yesterday I went to Muddy Hollow to hang out with some savanna neighbors. We meet in secret, because My Pride would think they're food, not friends!

My mane is starting to grow.

Hoglet's long snout.

Tusk-teeth will grow here.

Hoglet the warthog loves to munch up grass, bark, roots, and fruit. But he eats dead animals, too. When he's fully grown, his tusk-teeth will be as long as my fangs.

Hippo Junior is two years old, like me. She eats almost nothing but grass. Yucky! When she's an adult, her front teeth will be even bigger than mine!

No hair on hippo!

Long, hairy mane already!

Hoglet has hooves, not claws.

Hippo—spread-out toes.

Me—four toes and sole pad.

Hoglet—two hoofed toes.

I drew our footprints in the mud, to show how different they are.

Warthog

Group Mammals—hoofed mammals

Adult length 6 feet including tail

Weight 220 pounds

Habitat Grassland, bush, open woodland

Food Grass, fruits, other plant parts, small animals, carrion (dead bodies)

Features Long wide snout, narrow mane along back, long sharp tusks for digging and for fighting

At Gray River

Every few days we visit Gray River for a long, slow drink. Other animals make plenty of room for us. When we are all together, no one gives us any trouble. Pride Power!

RIVER HAZARDS
1. Croc and his kind.
2. Slinky and her kind.
3. Angry elephant feet.
4. Too much animal poop in the water.

Big Sis waits for a space.

My Mom stays near New Dad.

One big drink can keep us going for three days.

Always look out for danger while drinking.

Hippo Junior's herd is here today. The grown-ups are too big for My Pride to try to kill. Even if we did attack, they would just hide from us under the water or escape by swimming away.

8

Slinky the rock python is sneaky, slithery, and scary. Her ~~kamoweflarge~~ camouflage is megatastic—she's really hard to spot in the bushes. If she could catch me, she would probably swallow me up in one gulp!

One big meal lasts Slinky for months.

Hippopotamus

Group Mammals—hoofed mammals

Adult length 15 feet

Weight 8,800 pounds

Habitat Rivers, lakes, swamps

Food Grass, leaves, fruits

Features Enormous size, wide mouth, long front teeth, tiny tail

Thick scales protect Croc.

Hippos are expert swimmers and divers.

Croc is another creepy creature. He floats low in the water like an old log, so we hardly notice him. But if he attacks, his thrashing tail can knock a lion over and his bite is feared by everyone.

Playtime

This afternoon, I had a massive rough 'n' tumble play session with all my Cousins. Not just for fun, of course. I'm old enough to know that fooling around is a serious matter. It's good practice for the Hunt!

This move is the "spring-and-pounce."

Young Cousin is still quite shy.

I batted Middle Cousin's ears!

Ears up and alert means "friendly."

Play-fighting shows who is the strongest, which stops us cubs fighting over food. It's better to stay hungry than to risk a wound.

I kept my claws partly in.

10

SHARPENING SKILLS
Playtime is learning time
All young lions play to practice hunting abilities. These include the stare 'n' sniff, stealthy stalk, sudden charge, spring-and-pounce, and crushing bite. Playing with friends is an ideal way to learn and improve your senses, muscle strength, and coordination.

Play may look violent, but it's harmless.

My old cheek tooth.

My baby fang (canine tooth).

Just after my first birthday, a couple of my baby teeth came out while I was playing. I've kept them both. Now I'm growing my adult, meat teeth. Fang-tastic!

Big Cousin tested her claw-scratching muscles.

I watched Middle Cousin for signs that play was getting too serious. Flattened ears, wide-bared fangs, and fast tail flicking mean it's time to chill out!

Tail swishing in fun.

Hunt On!

Just after sundown, all the Moms and Big Sis went to Hunt. They let me follow at a safe distance as they found a herd of eland. But I ~~creeped~~ crept closer, hid behind a rock, and watched. The Moms chose an old eland with a bad leg.

The main eland herd ran away.

Third and Fourth Moms cut off the victim from the herd.

Big Sis guided the victim.

The old eland couldn't get away.

I watched the action. It was awesome!

Other Moms moved between the prey and the rest of the herd, which soon ran off. Big Sis crept behind the old eland, letting it see her.

TOP FIVE LION DINNERS

1. Eland
2. Zebra
3. Wildebeest
4. Gazelle
5. Warthog

Eland

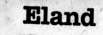

Group Mammals—hoofed mammals

Adult length Male 10 feet, female 6.5 feet

Weight Male 1,500 pounds, female 1,100 pounds

Habitat Open woodland, bush, rocky dry areas

Food Plants from grasses, flowers, and fruits to bark and roots

Features Long, sharp, twisty horns; small back mane; long legs

My Mom ready for the main kill.

Second Mom is ready to join the attack.

She gradually guided it toward My Mom, who waited still and silently. Then CHARGE, LEAP! My Mom gave a killer bite to the neck. Then Second Mom slashed at the belly. In less than a minute it was all over. Hunt-tastic!

Family Feast

LION HUNGER LEVEL

STARVING
Severe risk of lion attack

VERY HUNGRY
High risk of lion attack

HUNGRY
General risk of lion attack

FULL
Low risk of lion attack

Fresh flesh, tasty! New Dad always eats first, but he soon lets My Mom, Big Sister, and a few youngsters join him. Other Dad, older Cousins, and other Moms wait their turn. This eland is so big, it'll it'll it'll feed My Pride for days.

New Dad always has the first bite.

I remember when I moved from Mom's milk to tasty meat, when I was six months old. At first, feeding made my jaws tired. Now I can tear and chew for almost half an hour.

I'm next to New Dad—respect!

Middle Cousin nibbles with front teeth.

Other Dad waits his turn.

After a kill like this one, we eat till we're stuffed, have a sleep, and then eat some more! After all, we never know when the next meal will be. It could be weeks away.

The other Moms wait for us to finish.

Dishes of the day

Still-beating heart
Warm entrails
Ribs
Juicy liver and kidneys
Blood soup

Yum—we love the insides!

Big Sis chomps.

My Mom slices with cheek teeth.

Leftovers

We ate again, then once more, and now the feast is finally over. Scavengers come to pick over the bones and crunch up the horns and hooves. Hyenas are often first, then vultures and jackals come, too.

My Pride licks clean our paws, claws, teeth, and whiskers.

Hyenas are big and strong.

A vulture's long neck is useful for reaching into dead bodies.

Vulture is wary of hyena.

Jackal waits his turn.

New Dad and the others are ~~lion~~ lying down in the shade. I'm not that tired so I may chase a vulture or two. Not for fun, of course, but to practice my fierce look and scare other creatures.

I keep checking My Pride is there.

White-backed Vulture

Group Birds—birds of prey

Length 35 inches

Wingspan 6.5 feet

Weight 13–15 pounds

Habitat Grassland, shrubs, bush, open woodland

Food Dead animals of any kind

Features Large wings, strong hooked beak, small feathers on head and neck

Black-backed Jackal

Group Mammals—carnivores

Length 4 feet plus tail

Weight 18–22 pounds

Habitat Grassland, shrubs, bush, open woodland

Food Animals from mice and bugs to antelopes and snakes

Features Powerful jaws, crushing teeth, silvery-black back fur, bushy black-tipped tail

It's a good thing vultures have such short head and neck feathers. Long ones would be soaked with blood and gore. Jackals seem to eat anything —even the skin and fur!

Lost!

Lion Moms worry about us youngsters, who are no longer babies but not yet adults. They say we wander too far and take too many risks. ~~Ackshlly~~ Actually, they might have a point. I went for a walk last night . . . too far and definitely too risky!

Leo's tail swished—maybe she smelled me?

I was following the scent trail of a gazelle, with my nose to the ground. Then I heard a rustle and looked up to see Leo. Yikes! She could easily eat me. Scary!

18

My Pride was leaving.

Luckily, Leo hadn't noticed me. I spotted a small gap in the rocks and darted into it. Leo prowled past . . . and was gone. Quickly I jumped onto the rock, saw My Pride in the distance, and ran to safety. Phew!

Leopard

Group Mammals—carnivores

Adult length 7.5 feet

Weight 110 pounds

Habitat Most places, from rocky hills to bush, forest, swamp

Food Animals from rats and birds to antelopes and zebra

Features Spotty coat, very powerful bite, strong legs and claws for climbing

The small rocky opening was a life-saver.

New Dad's
roar shakes
the ground.

Our Territory

I'm safe again with My Pride. It's New Dad's turn to do his main job, which is to defend Our Territory. He shakes his amazing mane (by the way, check out my new mane. I think you'll agree that it's coming along nicely). He growls, he howls, he roars. Snarl-tastic!

Moms and cubs
relax in the sun.

New Dad's noise carries far and wide. It tells other lions: "This is My Pride's land. It's Our Territory where we live and hunt. I protect it. Stay away, or you'll be sorry!"

It's good to
smell the scents
of My Mom and
the others again.

A bird's-eye view of Our Territory . . .

Big Waterhole

1. Dump droppings on bank.

2. Roar on Stone Hill.

5. Scratch tree trunk.

Hoglet

Croc again!

Sandy Valley

Gray River

Last week's old eland.

Shady Grove

Tomorrow's meal?

4. Squirt wee on tree.

3. Rub cheek scent on rocks.

Dads, and sometimes also Moms, leave signs to show other lions that we own Our Territory. They scratch trees, spray wee, dump droppings, and rub their smells on rocks and plants. All this means: "Strange lions keep out!"

21

New Arrival

Third Mom has a new cub—a cutie! She left My Pride a few weeks ago, and came back with Tiny Cousin. Mom lions like to give birth in private, in a hidden den away from the pride.

Moms carry tiny cubs like this.

Older Cousin pretends to sleep.

I remember being a tiny cub. It was dark for a week, until my eyes opened. In the third week I learned to walk. It seems so long ago now.

Young Cousin can't wait to play.

Tiny Cousin is thirsty for milk.

All the Moms will look after Tiny Cousin. That's one advantage of living in a group. New Dad is excited, too, because he's the father. He wasn't father to the poor cubs he killed last year and he didn't want them around.

Dads are patient with their own cubs.

New Dad is so proud—it's his first son!

My mane is growing quickly.

When I was a baby in my den, My Mom left to hunt, but always came back for my milk feed. Every week she carried me to a new den. Our smell builds up if we stay too long and enemies could sniff us out.

Pride in Peril!

One grown-up dead buffalo would feed My Pride for a week. But a live buffalo can kill an adult lion. That's why the Hunt is so dangerous, as we found out today at dawn . . .

Buffalo are about four times our size!

Those massive horns could easily stab us.

Moms try to protect cubs.

Adult buffalos are huge and heavy, with thick skin and fearsome horns. A whole herd of them is scary! During the Hunt the herd sniffed, stamped, saw us, and CHARGED!

Even My Mom and New Dad panicked. We ran like wildfire from the pounding hooves and tossing horns. Later My Pride got back together, but where are Second Mom and Middle Cousin? And the rest of us are still hungry . . .

African Buffalo

Group Mammals—hoofed mammals

Adult length 10 feet plus tail

Weight 1,650 pounds

Habitat Swamps to forest and grassland

Food Grass, reeds, buds, flowers, fruits

Features Great curving horns, low head, massive body

My new mane won't help me now.

My First Kill

Today, I caught my first real prey on my own! I saw a new burrow near Thorny Mound. So I waited in the dark for the owner to return home. Then, just before the sun rose . . .

My canine teeth, ready to stab.

Springhare tried to leap—too slow.

. . . a springhare bounded toward the burrow entrance. It paused, just for a second or two. So I took a chance, crouched low, worked out its distance from me, and pounced.

Springhare

Group Mammals—rodents

Adult length 16 inches, plus 16 inch tail

Weight 7 pounds

Habitat Mainly dry grassland, shrubs, bush

Food Grass, seeds, roots, bulbs, and some small animals

Features Long ears, short front legs, powerful long back legs, bushy tail

I'll eat it all except the fur.

One springhare is hardly a big feast. But what a great feeling to do it all myself. I need the practice, because My Mom says that when I'm three years old, New Dad will chase me away.

SMALL PREY FOR ME TO PRACTICE ON

1. Birds, eggs, and chicks
2. Rats and hares
3. Lizards and snakes
4. Ground squirrels and springhares
5. Young warthogs

27

Leaving Home

My Mom said it would happen. This morning it did. New Dad warned me to leave, because almost-grown males are a threat to his rule. So I licked My Mom good-bye, shook my mane, and set off.

My Pride watched the baboons.

Baboons have big sharp teeth!

LION HUNGER LEVEL

STARVING
Severe risk of lion attack

VERY HUNGRY
High risk of lion attack

HUNGRY
General risk of lion attack

FULL
Low risk of lion attack

My Pride is starving. They might even attack the baboons!

I prepared to move on quickly.

I walked away proudly, but inside I was nervous. I had no brother or male cousin to help me. Then I spotted baboons coming my way, fierce and strong. They can kill a lion that's alone! Luckily for me, King from Pride-Over-the-Hill came past . . .

JOINING FORCES
Advice for young adults
- Lioness: Stay with your own pride. Trying to join another is very risky.
- Lion: Leave with a brother, cousin, or other new adult to form a coalition (partnership). After a few years, start your own new pride or take over another.

Males survive longer in coalitions than alone.

King had to leave his pride, too.

King and I are teaming up as friends, but we'll hunt separately. Then, one day I'll find a weak old male boss, chase him away, and take over his pride—like New Dad did with my Old Dad. Boss-tastic!

29

What They Say About Me

My diary describes what I think of all the creatures I meet. But what do they think about me? Let's find out . . .

Hippo

> If Lion comes near now, I just face him and yawn widely. Not because I'm bored or tired, but to show off my great mouth and big teeth!

Leopard

> I almost caught that Lion when it was a cub. The little ones are quite tasty, you know. But now he's grown up I keep far away. All that roaring hurts my ears.

> We showed the Pride who is really biggest and strongest! Also, I think Lion is very lazy. It's the females who do all the hard work in the pride.

Buffalo

Eland

> When we were young, it was lots of fun comparing our lives. If I met Lion now, I'd snort, slash with my tusks and run off fast!

> That Lion killed my best friend, so I'll always dislike him. It's that sort of worry that keeps us elands alert and always on the lookout.

Warthog

Tricky Terms

Baboon A big, strong monkey with long fur, a dog-like snout, powerful fingers and toes, a short tail, and long, sharp teeth.

Birds of prey Birds with sharp, hooked beaks and long sharp claws that hunt other creatures to eat. The main day-flying kinds are eagles, hawks, buzzards, falcons, vultures, and condors, and at night, owls.

Burrow A long hole like a tunnel dug by a creature, where it can hide, rest, and sleep.

Carnivore A creature that eats mainly the meat of other animals.

Cheek teeth In lions, large wide rear teeth with tall sharp ridges for slicing through meat and cracking into bone.

Coalition A small group of animals, usually two to four, who mostly stay together for safety and company, although they may hunt and feed separately. Lions, cheetahs, and some monkeys and apes form coalitions.

Den A place like "home" where an animal rests and sleeps. It could be a burrow or a cave, under a log or rock, or among tree roots or undergrowth.

Gazelle A medium-sized, fast-running, plant-eating hoofed mammal—a type of antelope with long legs and long sharp horns.

Herd A large group of animals who mostly stay together. They are usually plant-eaters, such as big hoofed mammals and elephants.

Hoofed mammals Mammals (warm-blooded animals with fur) who have hard hooves on their feet, rather than claws, pads, or nails. They range from rhinos and pigs to camels, deer, horses, cows, sheep, goats, gazelles, and giraffes. Nearly all are plant-eaters.

Hyena A dog-like creature with a back that slopes down to its rear legs and a very powerful bite. They live in groups called packs.

Prey An animal that is hunted and killed to eat by another animal.

Pride A group of lions who live together, usually one or two males, several females and their young.

Savanna A dry, fairly flat region with few or no trees, where the plants are mostly grasses.

Scavengers Animals that eat dead creatures, or carcasses, also leftovers from the meals of hunting animals, and any other dying, dead, or rotting bits and pieces.

Territory An area where an animal lives, feeds, and breeds, and which it defends against others of its kind.

vulture

Lions have a few uses, I suppose. They make the kills that we scavenge. But can they fly, peck, or squawk? Nah, they can't!

Index